A MONTH with SAINT FRANCIS

A MONTH with SAINT FRANCIS

Brother Ramon SSF

Illustrated by
MOLLY DOWELL

Published in Great Britain in 1999 by
Society for Promoting Christian Knowledge
Holy Trinity Church
Marylebone Road
London NW1 4DU

British Library Cataloguing-in-Publication Data

A catalogue record for this book is available from the British Library

ISBN 0-281-05272–7

Typeset by Pioneer Associates, Perthshire
Printed in Great Britain by
The Cromwell Press, Trowbridge, Wiltshire

For Michael Dowell

whose time and creative talents

have been given unstintingly to the Franciscan

brothers at Glasshampton Monastery

*

The royalties from this book will be donated to

The Cancer Resource Centre

at Kidderminster Hospital

CONTENTS

HOW TO USE THIS BOOK

This book is written plainly, to communicate some profound truths in a simple manner, so that it can be taken up and read in small doses, on a daily basis, or even right through, though the latter way would be less likely to yield the intended results.

Without wanting to dictate the way the reader wishes to use it, here are some guidelines which may be of value as they stand, or as they are integrated into an already existing prayer or meditation time.

- **Relaxation** Find a quiet place, sit in a relaxed but alert posture on a chair or prayer stool, with loose clothing, and shoes removed.

- **Respiration** Take note of your breathing without changing it. Then gently begin to breathe a little more deeply, slowly and regularly in an easy manner, from your diaphragm (tummy) rather than from the top of your chest. With this awareness slowly return to your normal rate of breathing.

- **Inspiration** Recall that the Holy Spirit is the breath of God, and open your body and mind to the Spirit's illumination as you prepare to read, using a simple spontaneous prayer, or repeating the verse:

  Breathe on me, breath of God.
  Fill me with life anew,
  That I may love as thou dost love,
  And do what thou wouldst do.

- **Reading** Take up the Franciscan meditation for the day, reading slowly and prayerfully through it, taking note of the illustration. Let this reading be rather like the sucking of a lozenge than the swallowing of a pill. Pause for reflection if a particular thought strikes you, and perhaps read it through a second time.

- **Resting** Rest within the love of God, allowing the theme of the day to be applied to your heart and mind by the Holy Spirit, with its implications for your daily life. Stay within that gentle state of prayerful waiting upon God for as long as it seems appropriate.

· **Conclusion** Gently move from the meditation to the reflective prayer, saying it audibly. After some silence, conclude the period with the blessing:

> *The grace of our Lord Jesus Christ,*
> *and the love of God,*
> *and the fellowship of the Holy Spirit be with us*
>   *all evermore.*
> *Amen.*

This simple method can be fitted into an already existing office of morning or evening prayer, or can stand on its own, with more time given to the resting and waiting parts, which will then make real God's promise:

> *Even youths will faint and be weary, and the young*
> *will fall exhausted; but those who wait for the LORD*
> *shall renew their strength; they shall mount up with*
> *wings like eagles, they shall run and not be weary,*
> *they shall walk and not faint.*
>
> (Isaiah 40.30–31)

A Month with Saint Francis

ST FRANCIS: UNIVERSAL BROTHER

St Francis called himself a 'friar minor', which means a 'lesser brother' of Jesus. And like Jesus, he lived as a brother to all creatures, loving the whole of creation and affirming the values of life, love and peace in a spirit of universal compassion – excluding no one. He lived only forty-four years, being born in Assisi in 1182 and dying there in 1226. And he left an indelible impression upon the world. I endeavour to be a lesser brother of Francis, and like him, I seek to live in the light of Jesus, with similar compassion, simplicity and joy. Our drawing illustrates one of my favourite sayings of Francis:

> Wherever we are, wherever we go, we bring our cell with us. Our brother body is our cell and our soul is the hermit living in that cell, in order to pray to God and meditate. If our soul does not live in peace and solitude within its cell, of what avail is it to live in a man-made cell?

I live in a wooden hut, in an enclosure in the grounds of Glasshampton monastery, Worcestershire; and I have friends who have erected simple meditation huts in their gardens. But Francis gets to the root of the matter: everyone has a cell – their body. Every man, woman and child should treat their body as a cell, with reverence and simplicity, not pampering it, but not (as he later realized) being cruel to it. The person who inhabits that cell of the body must live in creative joy, in praying and singing, and in praise of God. This positive life will overflow, bringing love, hope and peace to others.

A limited number of people come to my wooden hut, and they find such warmth inside that we are comforted together in the fellowship of our elder brother Francis, and most of all in the forgiveness and love of our greater brother and Saviour, Jesus. This is the basis of universal compassion and relationship with the whole of creation, as we shall see during this coming month. Will you share it?

REFLECTION

Lord Jesus, brother of all: you welcome all men, women and children to your arms, and embrace all creatures and the whole cosmos in your redeeming love. Brother Francis followed closely in your steps and became a brother to all. Let me begin anew, and like Brother Francis, allow your universal compassion to flow in and through my human life. Amen.

SSISI: DREAM CITY

Dreams can be wonderful – the hopes and promises of an imagination which yearns for fulfilment – or they can be nightmares. Assisi has been both. The nightmarish awareness of those who felt the strange climatic premonitions, and then the terrible experience of the series of earthquakes in 1997, will never be forgotten. And we still remember those who were killed and wounded. But today we think of Assisi as it has always been in our dreams, and as our illustration portrays it – a city set on a hill whose glory cannot be hidden.

You do not have to visit the holy place to revere it as the small city of Brother Francis. But what dreams were fulfilled for me many years ago when, as a parting gift, the congregation of St Mary's Episcopal Cathedral, Glasgow, sent me off to Assisi for two weeks! I was then considering a vocation to the Franciscan life, and that pilgrimage proved to be the stuff of which dreams are made.

I pitched my tent on the camping site of the Darmstadt sisters, halfway up Mount Subasio. This was an enchanting place because it was shared with pilgrims who were roughing it and living simply. At night, by the light of small fires, there was quiet singing, conversation and sharing within the camaraderie of the sisters and brothers of Brother Francis. It was a marvellous initiation into the Franciscan life.

We are now in the next century, but the memory remains as a dream fulfilled, and yet as a more profound and unfulfilled dream of the city of God, where Brother Francis leads us on in the company of all the sisters and brothers of Jesus. Our task is to plant the dream of Assisi, the city of God, the fellowship of love, wherever sin, darkness, injustice and human need are found in our fallen world.

Tumults and earthquakes threaten; the city of bricks and stone which Francis helped to rebuild will crumble in time. But the city we seek is not constructed of mortal and transient materials. It is built in the hearts of the sisters and brothers of Jesus the compassionate, and is eternal. And within that great multitude is our Brother Francis, leading his lesser sisters and brothers in simplicity and joy. For the kingdom of God is broader, wider, and deeper than any construct of the human imagination.

REFLECTION

Lord Jesus: as we dream our dreams, of which Francis and Assisi are part, grant that they may be translated into reality. Not bricks and stones, but penitent, obedient and loving hearts are the materials of your kingdom. You are its foundation, Lord Jesus, so let us build with joy and hope.

SACRO CONVENTO FROM A DISTANCE

Things often seem more beautiful from a distance. Indeed, we often need the perspective of distance when viewing a work of art, a place of architectural beauty or a natural landscape within its context of far horizon. But some things, and people, look better from a distance, because the nearer you get, the more disillusioned you become. Things are not always what they seem.

Assisi is not like that. And when the earthquake damage has been fully repaired, despite the loss of some irreplaceable treasures, it will shine once more with glory and wonder. My first sight of the beautiful small city from the railway station near the Portiuncula was enchanting. And it was not an illusion.

My entry into Franciscan life was not quite as enchanting. I needed to be *dis*illusioned, not only of the romantic habit, liturgy and lifestyle, but also of the 'community of love' which I had expected (and in some measure experienced) before I entered.

The losing of romantic and unrealistic illusions is essential. You have to accept people as they are, work at community, forgive and be forgiven as you live with your sisters and brothers at close quarters. But then . . . then the work of sanctification, reconciliation and simple human and humble forgiving love takes place. The distant scene takes on a new glory. I remember my first glimpse of Assisi and the Sacro Convento from a distance, and the ensuing joy I had in living within the city at close quarters.

I also remember my first entry, my disillusionment, and my second look at Franciscan life, at close quarters, from the inside. Today I have reason to thank God for Brother Francis, and for the sisters and brothers of all our three Orders, as well as the Companions. They have shared my enthusiasm for the Gospel; we have travelled together in our pilgrimage; they have supported me in my personal vocation; they have strengthened and sustained me in illness. Today I live in the simple but profound joy of both distance and closeness. With Brother Francis and my sisters and brothers, I travel closer to the holy city, and deeper into the divine love. It beckons from a distance, and encloses me in its warmth and eternal joy. Share it with me in our prayer today.

REFLECTION

Lord Jesus: from a distance your words and works fill me with wonder. As I draw nearer, there is a cross to bear and a discipline to follow. As you draw me closer to your heart of love I am enfolded, embraced and sustained by the love which led you to Calvary. Draw me nearer. Amen.

ENTER IN! A DOORWAY IN ASSISI

On one of her pilgrimages to Assisi, our illustrator Molly, who is a Companion of The Society of St Francis (SSF), and a Glasshampton neighbour, was taken with this simple but beautiful doorway in Assisi. When she showed me the drawing, we both felt that the whole symbol of the open door was so right not only for this book, but for our lives, influenced by Brother Francis of Assisi, and our share in the Franciscan life.

Molly finds it a great joy to sit in the streets and fields in and around Assisi, looking, observing, sharing and drawing. I found great joy, when I was there, in entering into the lives of ordinary people. On a bus to Spello one day, a feisty and ample Italian woman looked at my book *Italian Made Simple*, with its restaurant conversation about the different kinds of pasta. She was attracted, amused, amazed – and then with uproarious laughter, she took it from me, read it out to the passengers in the bus, and stunned me with a flood of Italian comments to which I responded with my fifteen phrases and thirty-seven remembered words! I obviously needed an Italian crash course at the wonderful university of Perugia. This was an open door into the warmth and humour of the ordinary people of Spello and Assisi. And I enjoyed it.

There is an open door for you today. First of all, there is an open door (if you are willing to enter) into friendship and conversation with ordinary people of all colours, classes, languages, religions and beliefs – on the simple basis of our universal common humanity.

Then there is an open door into the family of St Francis. It may be the right thing for you at this time. Both Molly and I have found a real joy and meaning in our lives within the Franciscan family, and within its Anglican form, there are four levels at which you may belong. (There is, of course, the larger Franciscan family within the Roman Catholic Church.) You could become a member of the First Order SSF as a full-time brother or sister, or be a sister of the Second Order of The Community of St Clare. If you protest that you have a family, a job, a set of responsibilities that does not allow you to consider such a full-time vocation, then you could become a tertiary, which is the Third Order with its appropriate disciplines. Or you could become a Companion of SSF, which is the simplest form of membership of the SSF family. But none of these is necessary to follow our Lord Jesus in the light of Brother Francis of Assisi.

Whatever your choice, there is an open door of opportunity for you today.

REFLECTION

Lord Jesus, door to the Father's heart: you are the door of salvation, and you place before me an open door of opportunity and service today. Let me become aware of it, and enter with you into newness of life and service. Amen.

THE BASILICA OF ST FRANCIS

Not long after this drawing of the basilica in Assisi was made, a great tragedy occurred. In September 1997, the *Daily Telegraph* reported: 'The upper basilica of St Francis and other historical buildings in and around Assisi are crumbling after the earthquakes' – and an accompanying picture showed scaffolding surrounding the basilica and a huge pile of rubble in front.

Many Franciscans and others around the world felt devastated by the destruction of the medieval churches and by the extensive damage to the priceless and unique paintings by the masters Giotto and Cimabue.

But many others recalled the attitude of the 'spirituals' among the Franciscan friars to the erection of the basilica and convent within two years of Francis's death in 1226. They were horrified by Brother Elias's costly architectural vision – a memorial to the simple man who had preached and lived poverty for himself and his friars. One day after Francis's death, Brother Leo ran to Brother Giles, who was living as a hermit near Perugia, crying, 'There is a marble vase set up at Assisi; and they throw money into it by order of Elias, to build a great rich convent for the brothers who have vowed to be poor like Francis!'

'Let them build a convent as long as from here to Assisi', replied Giles. 'My little nook is enough for me.' But Leo was not so passive. He made his way quickly to Assisi and smashed the vase with a hammer. Elias acted immediately: Leo was beaten with rods and exiled from Assisi.

Pilgrims of St Francis have been divided about the whole matter – on the one hand entranced by the amazing, beautiful and architecturally breathtaking basilica and convent of St Francis, yet on the other hand knowing that Francis and his friars of utter poverty are buried there, and recalling the complete radicalism of his life and preaching.

REFLECTION

Jesus, carpenter of Nazareth: the sacred buildings are being repaired; whatever can be done to restore some of Giotto's and Cimabue's art will be carried out, though much is lost. In the light of all this, let me remember that Brother Francis, following in your footsteps, had nowhere to lay his head, and help me to question the kind of life I live. Amen.

PILGRIM ARCHES

Today's drawing reveals some of the amazing symmetry and cohesion of the Sacro Convento from the vantage-point of the pilgrim arches. Whatever view we take of the value of architectural beauty, holy places, and the sacred space of pilgrimage, it can only be a source of sorrow that the disaster of the 1997 earthquakes marred the work of centuries-old creative genius.

It was not a madman who perpetrated such despoiling of architectural wonder – such as the one who attacked Michelangelo's white marble *Pietà* with an axe in St Peter's Church, Rome, in the 1960s. The Assisi episode was a natural catastrophe which caused me to tremble with strange fear when I saw it happen as filmed by the TV cameraman who was there at the very moment. The cries of '*Aiuto! Aiuto!*' sounded from the swirling dust which followed the collapse of the roof of the upper basilica. That image impressed itself upon me throughout the rest of the film which portrayed the painstaking work of the repairers and restorers on the artistic and architectural treasures.

In a typically Franciscan manner, it is a short step to consider the mortal dissolution of the human edifice of body and mind, symbolized by the destructive earthquake in Assisi. We have already noted that Brother Francis and his friars, in their day, lived simply in wooden and leafy huts with a few small stone buildings like the Portiuncula, which is now preserved in the huge basilica of St Mary and the Angels (see Day Twenty-Eight). And that Francis talked about his body being the cell in which the hermit lived.

All the physical beauty and attraction of our mortal frames will one day end in death and dissolution. This was especially true of those early pilgrims who travelled across Europe and slept around those pilgrim arches in Assisi. Life was shorter and more brutal in the thirteenth century, and the magnificence of the noble buildings in Assisi must have seemed eternal. Yet human mortality and natural catastrophe are part of our transient pilgrimage, and as pilgrim sisters and brothers of St Francis we must seek a more durable and eternal habitation beyond the confines of our earthly lives. We do not, nevertheless, despise earthly beauty, but treasure it the more – remembering to seek that city with eternal foundations, whose architect and builder is God (Hebrews 11.10).

REFLECTION

Jesus, fellow-pilgrim: the years of our pilgrimage make us increasingly aware that treasures of artistry and beauty, like the days of our mortality, come at last to dust. Teach me, as a true pilgrim, to journey through the world with compassion, to treasure the eternal qualities of love and peace, and to come at last to your heavenly kingdom. Amen.

BIRTHPLACE

Our drawing today depicts the birthplace of Francis in 1182. Roots are important to us all, and the places of birth and death are significant, though we have little say in either. Some years ago I went looking for the nursing home in Swansea where I had been born, and was amused to learn that it had later become a remand home for law-breaking boys!

It is not the geographical location of birthplace that shapes the person, and though the Franciscan pilgrim will want to linger and pray in the place of Brother Francis's birth, the search for Francis takes us further. Nikos Kazantzakis (*St Francis*, Oxford: Bruno Cassiver, 1962, p. 22) has Francis sitting in the winter sun at the tiny stone chapel of St Mary and the Angels, when a young pilgrim runs up to him breathless, and stands before him:

> 'Where is Francis, Bernadone's son?' he asked, his tongue hanging out of his mouth.
> 'Where can I find the new saint so that I may fall at his feet? For months now I have been roaming the streets looking for him. For the love of Christ, my brother, tell me where he is.'
> 'Where is Francis, Bernadone's son?' replied Francis, shaking his head. 'Where is Francis, Bernadone's son? What is this Francis? Who is he? I am looking for him also, my brother, I have been looking for him now for years. Give me your hand, let us go find him.'

In our quest for Brother Francis, every part of his life is significant, from birthplace to dying, and childhood is a good place to begin our search for him – and for ourselves. Do you know *where* you were born? Do you know *why* you were born? Has your search brought you nearer the spiritual and interior meaning of your life and identity?

The more we allow ourselves, like Francis, to be indwelt by the life and love of our elder brother, Jesus, the more we shall value the details of our own infancy and childhood, and discover that our true identity can only be found in the will and love of God.

REFLECTION

Lord Jesus, born in poverty: teach me to value my roots, the place and people of my birth and childhood. Then let me not remain there, but make the journey, as Francis did, following the steps of your humanity from earth to glory, so that the world may be a better place for my ever having been born. Amen.

THE CALL OF CHRIST

The little church of San Damiano, outside the old Assisi walls, was derelict and neglected. Masonry was loose, and there were holes in the roof. But the old crucifix was hanging, in Byzantine style, above the altar, and an old priest still said Mass there. The Christ-figure was not an agonized victim but the inviting Saviour with arms outstretched, as if he were saying, 'Come to me all you that are weary and are carrying heavy burdens, and I will give you rest' (Matthew 11.28).

It was to such a place that Francis came, inwardly moved by the Holy Spirit, and disillusioned with the knightly ambitions which had fired him earlier. He felt an inner voice telling him to go in and pray – so he obeyed. As he knelt before the crucifix he heard a tender and compassionate voice speaking to him: 'Francis, do you not see that my house is falling into ruin? Go and repair it for me.' Trembling and amazed, Francis replied, 'Gladly I will do so, O Lord'. And as he began to obey, he realized that a work which began with building stones and manual labour led to the building up of the lives of men,

women and children into the living temple of God, inhabited by the Holy Spirit.

There was a long journey ahead, and this moment of call was only the beginning of his conversion. His true conversion continued throughout his life and into eternity. So it is with us. We may experience a dramatic moment of conversion or an initiating call of the Holy Spirit, but that is only the beginning.

I mounted a large reproduction of that same Franciscan crucifix, and it hangs now above my altar-table in my hermitage chapel. I kneel before it every day in prayer and adoration of God. It represents to me, as it did to Francis, the crucified and risen Saviour who gave himself for me. I also realized that the early call to follow led into a whole lifetime of relationship – first as a saved sinner, then as disciple, evangelist, friend and lover of Jesus the Beloved One. So it goes on – deeper, fuller, and more significant each day. As with Francis, there are thorns as well as roses, but there is no other way for one who has been loved, called and filled with yearning for the Christ of God.

REFLECTION

Jesus, crucified and risen: when once you call there is no turning back; when once your voice sounds in the human heart there is no other voice to compare. Let your voice continue to speak, and let my heart continue to love and obey. Amen.

THE FIRST COMPANIONS

This is a beautiful picture. It marks the point at which Brother Francis realized that there would be other brothers. First, while spending the night in the wealthy home of Bernard of Quintivalle, Francis prayed in rapt contemplation through the hours of darkness. Bernard, who had watched his friend at prayer, was convinced of the reality of Francis's call, and asked to join him. In joy, they thought of the disposal of all Bernard's money and goods, so the next morning, joined by another brother, Peter of Catania, they went to St Nicholas's church near the main square in Assisi.

After prayer, they went to the altar and opened the gospel book three times, in devotion to the blessed Trinity. The first time it said: 'If you wish to be perfect, go sell your possessions, and give the money to the poor, and you will have treasure in heaven; then come, follow me' (Matthew 19.21). At the second opening they read: 'Take nothing for your journey' (Luke 9.3), and at the third: 'If any want to become my followers, let them deny themselves and take up their cross and follow me' (Matthew 16.24). At each opening they gave thanks, and

after the third gospel word, Francis said, 'O brothers, this is our life and rule and the life and rule of all those who may wish to join us. Go, therefore, and act on what you have heard.'

So off they went and distributed to the poor Bernard's great wealth and Peter's few possessions, aided by Francis who had already made such a sacrifice. Here were the first three brothers – companions in faith, for as Brother Francis afterwards said in his *Testament*: 'The Lord himself showed me that I should live according to the holy Gospel'.

Our vow of poverty is not as stringent – and there have always been difficulties in interpreting the literal following of that vow among Franciscans, especially if they have the care of schools, hospitals or churches. Some of them live in the midst of poverty in certain parts of the world, and others in a marketplace economy and culture of relative wealth in other parts. So poverty is interpreted, simplicity is enjoined, and all Franciscans should seek the basic, joyful and enthusiastic life of the early brothers. How about you?

REFLECTION

Jesus, brother of the poor: help me to look at my own life in its relative wealth and luxury, or in its relative poverty and simplicity, seeing it in the context of my church fellowship and the demands of the Gospel. Then inspired by your word, and by the simplicity and zeal of the first Franciscan brothers, let me take a step towards gospel values today. Amen.

ows

Whenever friars go into schools there is always great curiosity about our habit, and especially the three-knotted cord to symbolize the three vows. I often take along a spare habit, and get one of the taller girls to take the three parts (cross-shaped robe, hood, knotted cord), and clothe one of the taller boys in it, while I explain the symbolic meaning of each part. Some children know the monastic vows of poverty, celibacy and obedience, and sometimes look wide-eyed when they interpret them as 'No money, no marriage and no will of your own'! So we laugh together, and spell out what it means.

Poverty is not absolute. Today we have money to travel (though some of us hitch-hike) and for basic things, especially if we are involved in outside jobs, sometimes with salaries. Royalties from my writings go to the Provincial SSF Fund which is used inside and outside the Order. But we seek to live simply according to the culture in which we serve, and when we make our profession at the end of our noviciate we distribute any money or property we own.

Celibacy or chastity means different things for members of the First and Second Orders. It means no genital expression of sexuality for sisters and brothers of the First Order, but loving and chaste sexual relationships within lifelong commitment for Tertiaries and Companions, unless they feel drawn to a vow of celibacy. But in all this there is an encouragement to value the warmth and power of our sexuality, and to experience its positive channelling into creative acts and relationships in wholesome gospel living. The best of our humanity is suffused with our sexuality, and it is to be affirmed with joy.

Obedience is not into a monastic mould, or subject to a hierarchy or organization, but to the loving will of God, worked out within the community life, and in which both the community and the sister or brother give joyful assent, preferring the will of God to egotistic demands and preferences. When your will runs alongside the will of God, that is fine – but sometimes there is clear divergence. Then a decision has to be made, and sacrifice is involved on both sides. The basic affirmation is that in the will of God is our peace and true fulfilment: 'Not my will, but yours be done' (Luke 22.42).

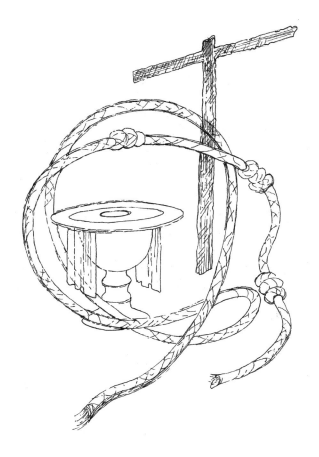

REFLECTION

Jesus, obedient to the Father: whether I wear a three-knotted cord or not, help me to understand the positive value of vowing my life to your love and service. Keep me faithful to my promises to you, as you are faithful in your covenant promises to me. And let your will be done. Amen.

SISTER CLARE: FELLOWSHIP IN FIRE

If you look closely at today's drawing you will see that Brother Francis and Sister Clare, rapt in prayer and conversation about the love and mercy of God, are surrounded by the divine fire which enfolds them in the forest surrounding St Mary of the Angels.

It is a marvellous story, and begins when Francis (who was very careful about his relationship with women), became convinced that it was time that he and Clare should meet together over a meal, to share what God was doing in and through them in the building up of the Franciscan community of love. The meal was prepared on the bare ground, but Francis and Clare entered into such a dialogue of glory and wonder that the food was forgotten, and the sisters and brothers around were caught up in its fiery joy. This is how the early Franciscan collection, *The Fioretti*, reports it:

> While they were sitting there, in a rapture, with their eyes and hands raised to heaven, it seemed to the men of Assisi and Bettona and the entire district that the Church of St Mary of the Angels and the whole place and the forest . . . were all aflame and that an immense fire was burning over all of them. Consequently the men of Assisi ran down there in great haste to save the Place and put out the fire, as they firmly believed that everything was burning up.

(Celano, 'The Fioretti', Marion A. Habig (ed.), *Omnibus of the Sources for the Life of St Francis*, Chicago: The Franciscan Herald Press, 1973, p. 1333)

When they arrived they found no material flames, but the fire and glory of the Lord, and they withdrew with a profound sense of awe and blessing. Fire, the symbol of the divine love, as the *Fioretti* affirms, was the conflagration of the Holy Spirit, and it spread around so that others were caught up in its light and warmth.

REFLECTION

Jesus, aflame for God: let me be drawn closer to the warmth of your love and the radiance of your joy, to the heat of your zeal for the salvation of the whole world. Let me burn out for you, Lord, and let your fire spread – from my heart, my family, my church, my neighbourhood and out into the world. Amen.

SAN DAMIANO: THE CLOISTER GARDEN

Here is the beautiful cloister garden at the church of San Damiano, where the crucified Christ called Brother Francis to serve him. It was here, towards the end of his life, that Sister Clare and her sisters cared for Francis when he was sick, blind and very weary.

One day, in extreme need, he cried out, 'Lord, help me in my infirmities that I may have the strength to bear them patiently!' And quite suddenly, he heard in his spirit the voice of the Lord assuring him of his loving care, and saying, 'Be glad and joyful in the midst of your infirmities and tribulations: as of now live in peace as if you were already sharing my kingdom.'

So it was that the next morning, though blind and weak, he composed *The Canticle of the Sun*, 'All creatures of our God and King . . . ,' and called upon the musical Brother Pacificus to sing it with some friars, and then to take it into the world as minstrels of the Lord. This happened at San Damiano's cloister garden, and brought profound consolation to Francis in the months before his death.

Sometimes, it is when we are in darkness and weariness that the Lord draws us to his heart in comfort and rest. It was out of such darkness that this most beautiful Canticle emerged, and has shed its light and glory in the world for eight centuries. And so it goes on . . .

REFLECTION

Jesus, Sun of Righteousness: I recall what Brother Francis said of the Canticle:

> *At sunrise, everyone ought to praise God for having created this heavenly body which gives light to our eyes during the day; at evening, when the night falls, everyone ought to praise God for that other creature, our brother fire, which enables our eyes to see clearly in the darkness. We are all like blind people, and it is through these two creatures that God gives us light.*

Santa Chiara on a Hill

Here is a view of Santa Chiara church from an unusual perspective, drawn before the 1997 earthquake caused the whole hill to tremble and damaged that precious building. As we have said, it strikes a warning on a material and spiritual level as we reflect upon our lives.

When I first entered this lovely church, before I became a Franciscan friar, I was stunned to see that the very crucifix which spoke to Brother Francis at the church of San Damiano was now housed in this church, dedicated to St Clare. This bears a mystical and symbolic meaning which was suggested to me then, and which has become more real and precious since I have been drawn into the life of prayer in solitude.

It means that the evangelical call, represented by the crucified Christ at San Damiano, and its summons to follow Jesus through penitence, faith and forgiveness, has now a more profound context – that of the contemplative life represented by St Clare and the church of Santa Chiara, now housing the crucified Jesus in his ancient and contemporary glory.

My life has evangelical roots, with fervent zeal, burning love and a deep desire to share the good news of the Gospel. And increasingly it is sustained by its contemplative depths which feed these roots – depths which have to do with the deeper reaches of prayer, compassionate intercession for a lost and needy world, and the adoration of God who calls the whole world into loving union with himself. The San Damiano cross above the altar in Santa Chiara church says it all in symbolic simplicity.

REFLECTION

Jesus crucified and glorified: you call me from my sins, from my attachments to the transient values of the world, and from my egocentric selfishness. You call me from the depths of your Spirit to the depths of my own – and I yearn for your love. Continue your evangelical and contemplative work in my life, and in the lives of those with whom I have fellowship in the way of Brother Francis and Sister Clare. Amen.

ASSISI ROOFTOPS

As Molly walked through the streets of Assisi, she looked up and looked down, and the next two drawings reveal something of the beauty she saw in the very ordinary but ancient loveliness of the tiny city loved by Brother Francis. Today's drawing immediately calls to mind Psalm 121:

> I lift up my eyes to the hills –
>> from where will my help come?
> My help comes from the LORD
>> who made heaven and earth.

In spite of the simple beauty of the place, the people, and the gentle bustle of Assisi, it is impossible not to look up – to see the lines of the buildings, the towers of the churches, and the weathered colouring of the roof-tiles. But then your eyes are lifted higher – to the ascending Mount Subasio where the Carceri is built into the mountain, and up again into the wide glory of the skies above Assisi.

This is a rooftop perspective in which the believer is drawn ever upwards, with both feet on the ground of mortality and charity, but with the heart in heaven. This is the pattern of Jesus who came from glory to Bethlehem, Nazareth and Galilee, and who indwelt his servants Francis and Clare in the streets and fields of Assisi.

Can it be that this is what God asks of us today – that he become incarnate in our life, in our town, where our feet are firmly grounded in the necessary business of family and social life, so that heaven may touch earth, as in the days of Jesus, Francis and Clare?

REFLECTION

Jesus of the rooftops: wherever we look, you are there! I raise my eyes and heart today above the worries and anxieties of marketplace life, and breathe the pure air of prayer and love. But let me not remain there, Lord. Come with me into the streets, lanes and fields where you are incarnate among the children of earth. Amen.

39

ASSISI STREETS

If you sit still and look at today's drawing you will first of all catch the sense of stillness which it communicates with its series of steps, rising ground, doorways, foliage and invitation to ascend and pass under the arching stones. Then you may feel that around that top corner, or through the doorway on the right someone will emerge: a man carrying the tools of his trade; a woman laden with vegetables, pasta and wine; a few children dancing, skipping, singing and running together; a poor beggar in ill health, hoping for your look of compassion or your deed of encouragement and help. Anything could happen – for this is a street in Assisi.

Are we as aware, as expectant, as open to other human beings, as we walk the streets of our village, town or city today? In Assisi you may not be surprised suddenly to come across a preaching friar, and even Brothers Francis, Bernard and Peter giving away their possessions would not surprise you unduly. Even in today's Assisi the commercial aspects of a holy place do not seem too outrageous, for there even pilgrims' purchases take on a certain charm and simplicity. The place dictates the style.

In one street I found a tiny shop full of local pottery, and purchased a goblet and plate which became a chalice and paten for the Eucharist. And it was there that I, a teetotaller, sat down under an Assisi awning, and drank a glass of the local wine – a novel experience for me, though I cannot comment on its quality!

REFLECTION

Jesus, Son of Man: as I move about my family and daily business today, make me aware of my surroundings, of my fellows, of the joys and needs of ordinary human life. Let me recognize the Christ-life in the people with whom I speak and share, and let your beauty shine through our humanity. Amen.

BROTHERS AND SISTERS

'A heavenly love can be as real as an earthly love', said G. K. Chesterton, speaking of the relationship between Francis and Clare. Today's illustration is a symbolic representation of Clare taking her vows, marked by Francis cropping her hair. Behind Clare are the sisters who would follow her into the gospel life, and behind Francis are the men who would follow him into the penitential Order which was causing such a revolution in Assisi. Julien Green, in *God's Fool* (London: Hodder and Stoughton, 1986, pp. 143ff), surrounds the story of Clare's calling with a romantic aura:

> When Francis was preaching in the cathedral of San Rufino, he had no idea that a young girl, seventeen years old, accompanied by her mother and sister, was listening with passionate attention to the great seducer of souls who spoke of God's love. Francis was not what is called handsome, and he was twelve years older than she. But that didn't matter because, as unsurpassingly beautiful as she was, she welcomed each of his words with an indescribable emotion. He wrenched her out of herself. Together with him she fell in love with Love – and how can you separate Love from love for Love's messenger? Had the two kinds of love interfused? We have only one heart to love God and his creatures. If Clare had been told that she was in love with Francis she would have been horrified and would not have understood. But after she got home, his voice, at once gentle and vehement, kept following her, preaching penance, scorn for riches, mortification of the flesh.
>
> She could no more resist the impulse to love than he could. It was their nature, hers and his, but this was the first time she had heard him extolling Love, and he revealed to her that their passion was the same: the infinite desire to be one with God.

Their relationship was human, wholesome, loving, and their disciplined lives always kept it so. Such discipline kept them free from a romantic or sexual attachment, and capable of such rare spiritual vision and experience as shown in the story of transformation in fire recounted on Day Ten. We are called by the same Love, and that calling suffuses our human loves, making us more loving, more compassionate, more human and gentle if we will but yield ourselves to it in faith.

42

REFLECTION

Jesus, lover of souls: you call us to the divine love of God, and you teach us that to surrender to this love is not to deny, but to enhance our human loves. Enable me to understand that as I love my sisters and brothers on earth more truly and profoundly, so will my love for God be deepened, and your fire be manifested in the warmth of my humanity. This is a great mystery, but I long to love you, Lord. Amen.

PRAISE AND ECOLOGY

St Francis not only acknowledged God as Creator, but experienced the presence of the divine love at the heart of the created order. He was not a pantheist and did not worship nature, but he discerned the vitality and glory of God in and through the natural world. Francis's genius was that he recognized and communed with the tenderness of God in nature's beauty and vulnerability.

One day, travelling through the Spoleto valley, he came across a great host of various kinds of birds. Leaving his companions, he ran towards them and greeted them with great joy, and they stayed, waiting expectantly. He was deeply moved and preached them a homily:

> My brothers and sisters, you should praise your Creator very much, and always love him; he gave you feathers to clothe you, wings so that you can fly, and whatever else was necessary for you. God made you noble among his creatures, and he gave you a home in the purity of the air; though you neither sow nor reap, he nevertheless protects and governs you without any solicitude on your part.

(Celano, 'First Life of St Francis', 58, Marion A. Habig (ed.), *Omnibus of the Sources for the Life of St Francis*, Chicago: The Franciscan Herald Press, 1973, p. 278)

At this, they stretched their necks, extended their wings, opened their mouths and gazed at him. Francis passed among them gently, touching them with his habit, and then he made the sign of the cross over them, blessed them and gave them leave to fly away. This whole episode stirred up deep reverence and joy among his companions.

It is at this personal level that ecological awareness and responsibility begin. If there is no loving awareness, no creaturely compassion, no relationship with nature and creatures – including all sentient beings – then there can be no genuine and lasting ecological concern. Brother Francis is the worthy patron saint of ecology for our day.

REFLECTION

Jesus, brother of creation: you manifested, in the simplicity and humanity of Francis, a love for nature and the animal creation, symbolizing a return to the paradise of Eden. Help me to learn such simplicity and humility. Let me also stir up among others a concern for all sentient beings, including a compassionate attitude towards the stewardship of wild and domesticated animals. Amen.

SPREADING THE NEWS

Today's illustration reminds us of the way in which Brother Francis followed Jesus literally, even in sending out the friars two by two to proclaim penitence and the good news of God's love. But Francis's evangelism was not aimed at damning people to hell for their sins, but rather at allowing the radiance and warmth of Christ's love and joy to shine from the friars' lives. This kind of gospel life drew people to Christ in confession of their own need and emptiness, and in yearning to know the forgiveness and peace which the friars so evidently possessed.

One day, a Dominican friar, a reputable doctor of divinity, visited Francis at Siena. He quoted Ezekiel 3.18: 'If you do not speak to warn the wicked from their wicked way . . . their blood I will require at your hand'. Then he told Francis that he knew of many who lived in mortal sin, but he did not always proclaim their wickedness to them, and he asked if Francis thought that their souls would be required at his hand.

At first Francis said that he was uneducated and unworthy to interpret such a powerful scripture. The Dominican replied that he had heard many learned men expound it, but he longed to hear Francis's understanding of the matter. So Francis yielded, and said:

> I would take it that the servant of God should be so aflame in his life and his holiness that he would reprove all wicked men by the light of his example and by the words of his conversation. So the splendour of his life will proclaim to all their wickedness.

> (Celano, 'Second Life of St Francis', 103, Marion A. Habig (ed.), *Omnibus of the Sources for the Life of St Francis*, Chicago: The Franciscan Herald Press, 1973, p. 447)

The Dominican was not only edified but amazed at such a definition of true evangelism, and he exclaimed, 'My brothers, the theology of this man, based upon purity of life and contemplation, is a soaring eagle; but our learning crawls on its belly on the ground.'

Such a humble attitude to evangelism is clearly manifested in the simplicity of today's illustration. Two humble friars with a donkey go begging their way from town to village, sometimes preaching, sometimes working manually, sometimes helping or conversing, sometimes silent, but always praying and in communion with their dear Lord. So the Gospel is proclaimed, and so people are won to the Saviour. Is that our kind of evangelism?

REFLECTION

Let the beauty of Jesus be seen in me;
All his wondrous compassion and
*   purity;*
Holy Spirit divine, all my nature
*   refine,*
Till the beauty of Jesus is seen in me.

THE WOLF OF GUBBIO

The Franciscan stories have many references to the fear of wolves, and to Francis's way with wild as well as domestic animals. The story of the wolf of Gubbio has captured the imagination, and our illustration depicts the wolf's ferocity as well as Francis's godly courage.

In the *Fioretti* the story is set in Gubbio, and the wolf's reputation was of sharp teeth and raging hunger, so that people would not venture outside the city at night. When they heard that Francis intended to confront the wolf, they cried, 'Look out, Brother Francis! Don't go outside the gate, because the wolf which has already devoured many people will certainly attack and kill you.'

But Francis signed himself with the cross and recalled the Lord's promise to protect him from the lion and the dragon. Soon he came to the wolf's lair, and it came running towards him with mouth open wide. Francis made the sign of the cross, saying, 'Come to me, Brother Wolf. In the name of Christ, I order you not to hurt me or anyone.' The wolf came, closed its mouth and lay at Francis's feet.

At this point, Francis preached a little homily, telling the wolf that his cruel and wicked ways deserved punishment, and that the whole town was outraged and was calling for justice. He went on to say that he was willing to act as mediator for forgiveness and peace, and the wolf moved his body, tail, head and ears, indicating that he would accept Francis's judgement.

So a deal was done. The wolf was to have sufficient food left each day if he would promise not to hurt animal or human being. Paw was put into hand, the pledge was given, and Francis took the wolf to Gubbio's marketplace where it was all confirmed. A sermon was preached to wolf and people. There was repentance, faith, promises, and praise to God from everyone. It's a marvellous story and should be read fully in the *Fioretti*. It concludes with the people mourning the death of Brother Wolf two years later, and with praise to Christ that such holiness and reconciling peace was revealed in Francis's life and witness.

True story or parable, it has a great deal to teach us about ourselves, about our communities and about our attitudes to creatures of the wild. Think it through!

REFLECTION

Jesus, Lion of Judah: you are fierce and gentle, stern and loving, full of strong discipline and joyous spontaneity. Enable us to deal with the wolf in our own human nature, to learn the ways of reconciliation and peace, and to live in joy and harmony with people and animals, as did our Brother Francis. Amen.

Mountain hermitage

This is a beautiful drawing of the *carceri* or hermitage on the slopes of Mount Subasio as it is today – one of the many Franciscan hermitages dating from the beginnings of the Franciscan adventure. Francis himself longed to live a life of prayer in solitude, but he was also pulled in the direction of communicating the Gospel by preaching and teaching.

Things came to a head one day when, with great longing for solitary prayer, he called Brother Masseo and sent him to Sister Clare at San Damiano and to Brother Sylvester, then a hermit at the *carceri*, who had a gift for contemplative prayer. Masseo was to ask them both whether it was God's will that Francis should devote himself entirely to prayer, or that he should sometimes preach. At this time numbers were increasing and Francis was beset by a situation in which he longed to be alone with God.

Off went Masseo, first of all to ask Clare to pray. Then he climbed up to the *carceri*. Upon hearing the dilemma and presenting the matter before the Lord, Sylvester was clear that Francis should continue to preach Christ and reap a harvest of souls. Masseo returned to Clare who told him the same thing, so he went quickly back to Francis at the Portiuncula.

Francis received him with humility, washed his feet and fed him. Then they went into the woods, and Francis knelt down before Masseo, bared his head, his arms in a cross, and asked, 'What does my Lord Jesus Christ order me to do?' Brother Masseo replied that both Clare and Sylvester had prayed and agreed that 'He wants you to go about the world preaching, because God did not call you for yourself alone but also for the salvation of others'. The *Fioretti* concludes powerfully:

> Then the hand of the Lord came over Francis. As soon as he heard this answer and thereby knew the will of Christ, he got to his feet all aflame with divine power, and said to Brother Masseo with great fervour: 'So let's go – in the name of the Lord!'

REFLECTION

Jesus, sent by the Father: let me not be hasty in deciding what is your will for life's decisions. Give me the humility to seek the prayers of fellow-believers and loved ones. Make me more aware of the communion of saints on earth and in heaven, and that we are linked together in prayer and love, to do the will of our heavenly Father. Amen.

THE THIRD ORDER FAMILY

Following from yesterday, when Brother Francis heard what Masseo had communicated – that he should continue his preaching – he took him and Brother Angelo, 'and set out like a bolt of lightning in his spiritual ardour', and soon arrived at Cannara. His preaching was surrounded by the accompaniment of twittering swallows, and he was so fervent that the whole village turned out, and wanted to abandon Cannara to follow him. 'Don't be in a hurry', he said. 'I will arrange what you should do for the salvation of your souls.' And from that time, says the *Fioretti*, he organized the Third Order for the salvation of people everywhere.

There were many liberating aspects for people who became part of the Franciscan family as Tertiaries, in families and groups. Two of the most important elements were the commitment to reconciliation – that is, not taking up arms – and freedom from the oath to a suzerain or *commune*. There were political repercussions to these, of course, but they did affirm the personal and religious liberty of Tertiaries, and were an amazing application of the Gospel to their individual and social lives.

It was at Florence in 1221 that the first Fraternity of Tertiaries was established, and from there the Third Order spread all over the world, and included royals like St Louis of France and St Elizabeth of Hungary, former sinners like Margaret of Cortona and Angela of Foligno, children like St Rosa of Viterbo, and illustrious people such as Petrarch, Michelangelo, Dante, Murillo, Christopher Columbus, Palestrina and Liszt.

In our day the gentle but powerful influence of Tertiary Archbishop Desmond Tutu continues to work as leaven in the conflicts and reconciliations of South Africa, and I am in touch with so many of our own local Tertiaries. Immediately there come to mind those who are reading along with me through my Lent book this year, and the Cornish Tertiaries who sustained me in love and prayer during my recent illness. In Christ, the Franciscan family continues in loving service.

REFLECTION

Jesus, elder brother: thank you for all those who have been touched and set aflame by the witness of Francis. May his simplicity, love and joy shine like a radiant beacon through the materialism and corruption of our world, beginning in my life. Amen.

BROTHER OF ALL

Up in the *carceri* on Mount Subasio stands a statue of Brother Francis and a child – the subject of our drawing today. This simple, fraternal relationship is found in the context of the natural world, and in a place set aside for prayer and solitude.

I used to love going into schools before I began my hermit exploration, and I well remember the day the Methodist Junior School in Canterbury set aside a whole 'monastic day'. The pupils made their own habits which they wore for the day, and they did the garden work, cooking, calligraphy, hospitality and offices of prayers and readings which the monks and nuns would have done in their place. The crown of the day came when I knelt with them in the chapel, and took them through the repetition of the Jesus Prayer: 'Lord Jesus Christ, Son of God, have mercy on me, a sinner'. They learned it quickly, joining in with a wonderful sense of unity and corporate joy.

Children always respond to the Franciscan presence, and often shout humorous quips when we appear in public places. I remember one group, when I was on mission one Sunday evening, who asked me, 'What time are you frying tonight, friar?' I told them, and two of them came to Evensong where they took part by ringing the bell.

Perhaps it is a long way from that chirpy group to the leafy contemplative innocence of our statues at the Assisi *carceri* – but it is all of a piece, and the tradition of Franciscan spirituality affirms the presence of God in the wilds of nature, in the marketplace of commerce and in the sacred place of prayer. There is no person or creature who is outlawed from the loving concern of Brother Francis, for he was a true follower of Jesus who welcomed all to his kingdom of love and peace.

REFLECTION

*Jesus, friend of all: forgive me for
only wanting fellowship with those
of my persuasion, and only granting
friendship to those who qualify by
my standards. Give me a childlike
heart and a spontaneous spirit;
break down the barriers and
prejudices that I have erected over
the years, so that I may be brother
or sister to all. Amen.*

Dizzy Guidance

St Francis and Brother Masseo were travelling one day in Tuscany. They came to a crossroads with signs to Florence, Siena and Arezzo. 'Which road should we take?' asked Masseo. 'The road God wants us to take', replied Francis. But Masseo didn't think that this was much help.

Then Francis said, 'Masseo, I want you to do what children do. Start twirling around at this crossroads, and don't stop until I tell you.'

Masseo frowned for a moment, then saw the look in Francis's eye, and he obeyed. He twirled and circled, stumbled, fell and twirled again, until Francis shouted, 'Stand still! Don't move!' This was difficult, but Masseo managed it and said in a dazed sort of way, 'I am facing towards Siena'. 'Well that is the road God wants us to take', replied Francis, and he set off confidently, with Masseo following behind.

As they went, Masseo thought to himself that Francis really did do some stupid things sometimes. What on earth was the use of twirling around like a child,

especially as he had been conscious that some layfolk had passed by and stared at his childishness.

When they got to Siena, some people came out to meet them with joy. They took Francis and Masseo to a group of Sienese citizens whose domestic quarrels had turned into bitter fighting, and two of the men had been killed – which made matters even worse.

Immediately Francis stood in the midst of the squabble, and his simplicity turned into authority. He preached earnestly on the stupidity and uselessness of violence, and such was the inspiration that flowed from him that the people's hearts were moved, tears flowed, and penitence and reconciliation followed.

As they continued their journey the next day, Masseo said to himself, 'Thank God for Brother Francis. My respectable behaviour and my sensible decision would have taken us on the wrong road, and what a blessing I would have missed. If I am to enter the kingdom of God, I must become like a little child.'

REFLECTION

I know I must be responsible and mature in my actions, Lord, but help me also to be childlike, open, playful and pliable in your hands. Perhaps you have a task for me today, so help me to experience the sheer joy of being abandoned to your will, and let that joy overflow to other lives. Amen.

TOTAL COMPASSION

We said yesterday that Francis was a brother to all. It is not difficult to substantiate that statement from the many wonderful stories of his openness to all sorts and conditions of people – especially to the colony of lepers near Assisi and on the roads of Umbria. He warned nobles and peasants alike that if they wanted to join the Order, they would have to work at the leper house.

Today's drawing depicts one of my favourite stories. This particular leper had exasperated the friars who had tried to help him – he was belligerent, impatient and violent, cursing both them and Christ, so that they concluded that he was possessed of an evil spirit.

Francis therefore went to him saying, 'God give you peace, my dear brother'. The leper retorted, 'What peace can I have from God who has taken from me all peace and everything that is good, and has made me all rotten and stinking?' The poor leper had come to an end of himself. And then the transformation took place.

Francis looked, listened, loved, and began his work. He boiled water with sweet-scented herbs, undressed the man and washed him all over with tenderness, simplicity and prayer. The story says that wherever Francis touched him, the flesh began to take on a new appearance – and at the end of the bathing, the man was healed.

As the leper's body was healed, so his tears flowed, and repentance was mingled with sorrow, grief and gratitude – to Francis and to God. His body was cleansed with water, his conscience with tears, and his sins with the blood of the Saviour. 'Woe to me', he cried, 'for I deserve hell for the insults and injuries I have given to the friars and for my impatience and blasphemies against God.'

Two very different figures of our day died in the same week a few years ago – Mother Teresa of Calcutta and Diana, Princess of Wales. The first gave her whole life in ministry to the abjectly poor, ill and dying. The second, in spite of the equivocation about her life, took hold of the hands of brothers suffering from AIDS. Both reflect the spirit of Francis and Jesus. In what ways do our lives manifest such a spirit of empathy, with hands extended in genuine service?

REFLECTION

Jesus of the loving heart: the leper ran to you saying, 'If you choose, you can make me clean'. Immediately you reached out and touched him, saying, 'I do choose. Be made clean!' Inspire my life today with such compassion, and let your healing love flow through me. Amen.

MYSTERIOUS LA VERNA

There are some places which have a sense of mystery and awe about them, made sacred or sinister by holy or demonic deeds, hallowed by prayer or desecrated by evil – and it can be felt. There are also places where light and darkness mingle, and sometimes holy places have been sanctified on the sites of previous darkness or evil. I felt this conflict between light and darkness on the island of Bardsey, off the tip of the Lleyn Peninsula, when I lived there in solitude on the Anelog mountain during the winter and spring of 1983–84.

In the Franciscan story, such a place is Mount La Verna in Tuscany. Francis once preached so powerfully at Montefeltro that Count Orlando of Chiusi was converted, and made a gift of this mountain to Francis – who owned nothing else! It was there that Francis built a wooden hut on a small plateau.

One day, standing alone beside this cell, he gazed upon the form of the mountain with its chasms and massive rock openings, and he felt them to have been battered and split at the hour of Christ's passion when it was said that 'the earth shook and the rocks split' (Matthew 28.51). There are a number of these Calvary associations – one in Wales is called 'The Skirrid', and is known as the Holy Mountain of Gwent. These are 'thin places' where earth and heaven meet for those who seek the holy in the things of earth.

Tomorrow we shall consider that amazing episode which made La Verna especially sacred to Franciscans, but today we remember that on 30 September 1224, after attending Mass on the holy mountain, Francis commended its care to the Brothers Masseo, Angelo, Sylvester and Illuminato, saying:

> I desire that the Superiors only send here brethren who love God and are among the best of the Order. Remain here in peace, my dear children – *Addio!* As for me I go to the Portiuncula never to return. My body will be far from you but I leave my heart with you . . . *Addio!*

Masseo added to the account that they all wept warm tears as Brother Francis left them, weeping too, and carrying their hearts with him.

REFLECTION

Jesus of the mountain: you revealed yourself on the mountain of Transfiguration to your disciples, and on the mountain of La Verna to Francis and his companions. Let me today ascend in heart and mind to gaze upon your glory and be moved by your tears. Amen.

STIGMATA

Just before his death, Martin Luther King said, 'It doesn't matter now because I've been to the mountain . . . I just want to do God's will.' The mountain makes all the difference, and there is something about mountain experiences which draws the heart and mind to the high places of the spirit,* and so it is today with Francis on Mount La Verna.

What happened there was the stigmatization of Francis – the imprinting upon his hands, feet and side of the Calvary wounds of Jesus, indicating the mystical union between Francis and his beloved Saviour. We shall not today try to understand *what* happened, but consider the *attitude* of Francis to that mysterious miracle of grace.

There was a kind of inevitability about it, similar to that which possessed Jesus as he moved towards the cross. Father Cuthbert, the Franciscan biographer, speaking of the attraction, says, 'His spirit was drawn towards a rarer atmosphere'. This was not an ascetic and world-denying death wish, but a profound yearning for union with the divine Love. Francis never lost sight of the fact that beyond Calvary was the resurrection, and that dying with Jesus was a prerequisite to risen glory. The whole attitude is expressed in the prayer of Francis as he knelt near his hut before the eastern sunrise, on the Feast of the Holy Cross in 1224. It was total abandonment to the will of God, a physical, mental and spiritual surrender to the mystery that lay at the heart of Christ's love:

> 'My Lord Jesus Christ, I pray you to grant me two graces before I die; the first is that during my life I may feel in my soul and in my body, as much as possible, the pain which you, dear Jesus, sustained in the hour of your most bitter Passion. The second is that I may feel in my heart, as much as possible, that excessive love with which you, O Son of God, were inflamed in willingly enduring such suffering for us sinners.'
>
> (Celano, 'The Fioretti', Marion A. Habig (ed.), *Omnibus of the Sources for the Life of St Francis*, Chicago: The Franciscan Herald Press, 1973, p. 1448)

*Brother Ramon SSF, 1998, *The Prayer Mountain*, Norwich: The Canterbury Press.

REFLECTION

Jesus of Calvary: I cannot begin to understand the mystery that lies at the heart of the cross, or the complete surrender of Brother Francis to your suffering love; but grant me to know in part what it means, and to take one simple step nearer the cross today, so that your passion and glory may be manifested in my small life. Amen.

DYING WITH JESUS

It would be a mistake to take Francis's asceticism as the primary statement of his life and witness. His continued story, down to our day, has been one in which he is associated with simplicity, spontaneity and joy. Nevertheless it is true that naked he came into this world; naked he divested himself of his father's wealth and clothing at twenty-four years of age; naked he asked to be laid upon the bare ground as a preparation for his death in 1226.

We all have to acknowledge that we must die, but we spend so much of our time putting off or evading the truth, because we have not truly lived, have become too attached to the baubles of this world, or are too afraid to face our mortality. The thirteenth-century account, *Speculum*, reports the positive affirmation of Francis in the face of death. A friendly doctor, John Buono from Arezzo, is asked by Francis, 'What do you think about this dropsical disease of mine?' 'Brother', replied the doctor, 'God willing, all will be well with you'.

Francis would not be fobbed off: 'Tell me the truth', he persisted. 'Don't be afraid to tell me, for by God's grace I am not such a coward as to fear death. By the grace and help of the Holy Spirit I am so united to my Lord that I am equally content to die or to live.'

Then John Buono told him frankly, 'According to our medical knowledge your disease is incurable, and it is my belief that you will die either at the end of September or in early October'. Then, says the *Speculum*, the blessed Francis, lying on his bed, most reverently and devoutly stretched his hands to God, and with great joy of mind and body, said, 'Welcome, Sister Death'.

The *Speculum* concludes by heralding the dimension of eternity, no longer dwelling upon failing mortality, but in resurrection hope:

> After twenty years of perfect penitence, he departed to the Lord Jesus Christ, whom he had loved with all his heart, with all his mind, with all his soul, and all his strength, with the most ardent desire and with utter devotion, following him perfectly, hastening swiftly in his footsteps, and at last coming in the greatest glory to him who lives and reigns with the Father and the Holy Spirit for ever and ever. Amen.

> (Celano, 'The Speculum', Marion A. Habig (ed.), *Omnibus of the Sources for the Life of St Francis*, Chicago: The Franciscan Herald Press, 1973, p. 1265)

REFLECTION

Jesus, Lord of life: you travelled the valley of death into the light of eternity, and possess the keys of hell and death; our brother Francis followed the trail you blazed, and lives with you in glory. Save us from the fear of death, grant us dying grace when our time comes, and until then a ministry of love and prayer to the dying and the departed. Amen.

LEAVING ASSISI

The city gate in today's drawing looks down the road towards the basilica of St Mary of the Angels below Assisi, in which the tiny stone Portiuncula chapel is preserved. Any pilgrim will want to leave Assisi at some point by this gate to visit this holy place. We cannot stay forever on the Mount of Transfiguration or in the holy city of Assisi, and the time will come for us to go through this gate and return home to the places which we may think of as secular and unimportant.

Places are not inherently holy – they are made so by the numinous presence of the mystery of God. When God manifested his glory to Jacob at Luz, in the ascending and descending angelic ladder, Jacob wakes up and cries out:

> 'Surely the LORD is in this place – and I did not know it!' And he was afraid, and said, 'How awesome is this place! This is none other than the house of God, and this is the gate of heaven'. (Genesis 28.16–17)

The most wonderful thing about a pilgrimage is to return home and find that God was there all the time – hidden in the depths of our heart and among our neighbours. Yet the pilgrimage may have been necessary for us to perceive that truth. When I made that special pilgrimage to Assisi in 1976 I stayed for the first few days in an ecumenical institute, but it was so full of clacking typewriters and ringing telephones that it was a great relief to put on my backpack, and climb to the Darmstadt site halfway up Mount Subasio. It was there I pitched my tent, and with the pilgrims I found stillness, darkness, gentle camaraderie and a genuine Franciscan warmth around the open fire and under an open sky.

Assisi, and all holy places, are to be cherished in the heart, and if they do carry the heavy sense of the numinous presence of God they will also affirm the more profound reality, which is the Spirit's indwelling in the human heart.

Doorways in and gateways out. But the entrance to genuine spiritual life is Christ himself.

REFLECTION

Jesus, indwelling Saviour: unless you dwell within my heart, of what worth are pilgrimages to Assisi or any other holy place? You are the presence who makes the place holy – so let me evermore dwell within your love. Amen.

THE PEARL WITHIN THE OYSTER

This is a remarkable drawing, for it portrays the original, tiny stone chapel of St Mary of the Angels (called the Portiuncula), preserved within the immense and beautiful basilica of St Mary of the Angels situated on that road leading from Assisi. Portiuncula means 'little portion', and this little portion is also a little pearl within the huge oyster of the basilica which houses it.

In spite of what I said yesterday about sacred places not being inherently holy, this is certainly a place in which resides the spirit of Brother Francis in his simplicity and holiness. However, it is the reality of God's presence that validates that claim – and you have to be in tune to feel it!

When Francis began his discipleship by repairing churches, he started with San Damiano, then moved on to St Peter's church in Assisi, and went on down the road into the woods on the plain below, to this very place. He decided not only to repair the ruined stone chapel of St Mary of the Angels, but to settle there. Bonaventure tells us that he loved this spot more than any other in the world.

No one who makes a pilgrimage to Assisi will miss it. But the pilgrim may stand outside the tiny chapel, on the marble floor of the great basilica, and gaze around at the size, the splendour and the breathtaking beauty of the glorious building that houses Francis's tiny stone chapel. And standing there, may wonder what Francis would have thought of it all.

This little pearl confirms Francis's love of little things – simple, homely and humble things. It is not the fine building, but what is housed within it; not the fashionable clothes, but the person who wears them; not the beautiful body, but the spirit of love and generosity that personifies it. All this is confirmed by this tiny pearl within the basilica oyster today. 'The LORD does not see as mortals see; they look on the outward appearance, but the LORD looks on the heart' (1 Samuel 16.7).

REFLECTION

Jesus, pearl of greatest price: enable me to value inward truths and virtues, to see deeper than superficial wealth, know-how, adornment and decoration, to the hidden cave of the heart. Then I shall live from that secret place of the divine indwelling. Amen.

TRANSITUS: FROM EARTH TO GLORY

This strange drawing comes from our monastery chapel at Glasshampton, Worcestershire, when we remember Francis's 'Transitus' from earth to heaven, on the evening of 3 October each year. A habit is laid on the chapel floor before the altar, with five lights signifying the five wounds of Francis's stigmata. We begin the memorial with the words: 'Francis, poor and lowly, enters heaven rich', and we offer thanks for his journey from earth to heaven. There are Scripture readings and prayers, and during the solemn blessing the monastery bell is tolled forty-four times to mark the years of Francis's life.

All such symbolic acts are meant to lead us into a deeper consideration of the truths they set forth, and I find this one particularly moving. The word '*transitus*' has to do with transition, as in a journey, and transience, as in the sequence of time, which is also a journey. Forty-four years are not very long, though perhaps perceived differently by a twenty-year-old novice full of vitality and enthusiasm, and an eighty-year-old friar who may not have lost his enthusiasm, but feels the weight of mortality and the transience of human life.

I often commend Brother Francis to my non-Christian and humanist friends, for he has universal appeal as the saint who encapsulates all that is best in the Christian tradition. But it is difficult to make real sense of his life without recognizing his awareness of living in the light of eternity. Francis not only loved his Saviour in this life, but fully expected to be united with him in love beyond the frontiers of mortality and death.

And that is just what we celebrate in the memorial of the Transitus!

REFLECTION

Jesus, Lord of the living and the departed: you have conquered death and hell, and our hope in you is not for this life alone. Enable me to live my earthly life fully, compassionately, joyfully, but never let me lose sight of fullness of life beyond its mortal confines. Amen.

EARTHQUAKE!

The TV cameraman who was filming inside the upper basilica of St Francis after the first tremors in September 1997, was caught up in the main earthquake and roof fall. He filmed it as the roof fell in, clouds of rubble and dust filled the building, and cries of help were registered on the soundtrack. Here is a drawing of those first moments.

Whatever the Franciscan view of architecture, buildings, works of art and holy places, this was a devastating episode in the history of Assisi. Some people were killed, including two friars, and the reverberations still sound in the hearts and minds of those involved.

The mortal remains of Brother Francis and some of the first friars are secure in the lower chapel, and whatever he would have said about the earthquake, Francis would certainly have addressed the earthquake experiences of our lives. A loved one is involved in a fatal road accident; the child of a dear friend is dying of leukaemia; your father is suddenly felled by a massive stroke; your spouse is diagnosed with cancer; you suffer a paralysing coronary thrombosis.

These are not rare occurrences. They happen every day, and your life and family may be touched, or shaken to their foundations. Things can never be the same afterwards, even if your daughter now has a clear mammogram after breast cancer, or there is gradual recovery after that massive stroke. Our mortality has to be faced, our dying has to be confronted. When death touches us closely, we have to take it on board, truly grieve, and realize that our tears are not ours alone, but a share in the world's grief.

And before we sermonize about 'pie in the sky when we die' we have to be realistic about the earthquake which has invaded our lives or the lives of our loved ones. Take it seriously, deal with it humanly, experience it compassionately – in another's life or your own. It is the experience of earthquake.

REFLECTION

Jesus, friend in need: when earthquake experiences erupt in my life, let me not run to drugs, alcohol or regression in order to evade the real confrontation. Give me the inward strength and spiritual serenity to face whatever comes, knowing that I am not alone in my suffering, and that you will never leave or forsake me. Amen.

AFTER THE EARTHQUAKE

There is always the 'afterwards'. In our drawing today, it is the afterwards of restoration. The scaffolding inside the upper basilica stands in front of Giotto's precious fresco of Brother Francis supporting the whole Lateran Church as it threatens to collapse in ruins. This was the substance of the dream that caused Pope Innocent III to take Francis seriously.

The TV shot on which this drawing is based marvellously communicates the universal truths of ruin and restoration, the basic facts of our fallenness and renewal which are part of our physical, mental and spiritual lives.

Our 'afterwards' experiences involve us in a lifetime of rebuilding, and call forth the human virtues of patience, trust, faithfulness and humility. It means Saul of Tarsus getting up blind from the ground after the earthquake of his conversion, and allowing the Lord to remake his life after a new pattern; it means staying with the medical therapy which accompanies that life-threatening diagnosis; it means watching at the bedside of your loved one in intensive care, longing for signs of recovery and hope; it means being loving, tender and patient with yourself as you recover from the physical, mental or spiritual catastrophe which has devastated your life like an earthquake.

But in all these things – earthquake and restoration – you are not alone. Jesus is not only the Saviour who will forgive and renew your spirit. He is also your physician who will tend your wounds and comfort you in your affliction. He is your friend and elder brother who will walk beside you, allowing you to lean on him, sharing and bearing your burdens, and enabling you to communicate his strength and grace to others.

There is life after the earthquake. The work of restoration goes forward in Assisi, with all kinds of specialist architects, artists, restorers and builders having their place in the overall plan. In that invaluable work compassion and creativity flow – and in your life and mine!

REFLECTION

Jesus, physician and restorer: I look around me and within, at the earthquake experiences which have caused havoc in my life and the lives of those I love. Grant to me renewed hope as I seek to rebuild from the rubble of dashed hopes and frustrated energies. Give me patience with myself and others, so that your strength may enable, and your beauty shine forth at last in restoration. For today and for eternity. Amen.

FRANCIS AND THE NEW MILLENNIUM

What do you make of this last drawing? The thirteenth-century St Francis stands at San Damiano with the transient path of time leading through creatures and people, towards the Millennium Dome! One of our friars remarked that he didn't think Francis would be much interested in a Millennium Dome, and could have suggested some other uses for the money!

Perhaps he was right. But I do believe Francis would be there. Probably preaching outside, and possibly being arrested either for causing a disturbance or for the content of his message. It was at a knightly celebration that he leapt on to a wall at Montefeltro, and took his text from the romantic troubadour songs that they were singing. He seized the opportunity, and that was the day that Count Orlando was converted by his powerful preaching, and gave him the mountain of La Verna.

The fact is that thirteenth-century Francis has followed us into the twenty-first century, and has made real the Jesus of the first century with more relevance than ever. Brother Francis stands as a beacon in our world, for forgiveness and reconciliation, for simplicity and compassion in human life, for openness to every living creature, for ecological awareness and care of the natural order, and for solid and positive faith in a world of darkness, violence and doubt.

I don't know about you, but I take Brother Francis both as the patron saint of the Order to which I belong, and as a model for my human and Christian life. I follow him as he followed our Saviour, Jesus Christ. This is the note to conclude our month together, and if there is one thing that Francis would do, it would be to point us to Jesus, in order that we might hear his words, and accept his invitation of grace and love:

> 'Come to me, all you that are weary and are carrying heavy burdens, and I will give you rest. Take my yoke upon you and learn from me; for I am gentle and humble in heart, and you will find rest for your souls. For my yoke is easy, and my burden is light.' (Matthew 11.28)

REFLECTION

The Franciscan greeting is 'Peace and Blessing!', but let's repeat it in friendly Italian: Pace e Bene!

The Society for Promoting Christian Knowledge (SPCK) was founded in 1698. It has as its purpose three main tasks:

- **Communicating the Christian faith in its rich diversity**

- **Helping people to understand the Christian faith and to develop their personal faith**

- **Equipping Christians for mission and ministry**

SPCK Worldwide serves the Church through Christian literature and communication projects in over 100 countries. Special schemes also provide books for those training for ministry in many parts of the developing world. SPCK Worldwide's ministry involves Churches of many traditions. This worldwide service depends upon the generosity of others and all gifts are spent wholly on ministry programmes, without deductions.

SPCK Bookshops support the life of the Christian community by making available a full range of Christian literature and other resources, and by providing support to bookstalls and book agents throughout the UK. SPCK Bookshops' mail order department meets the needs of overseas customers and those unable to have access to local bookshops.

SPCK Publishing produces Christian books and resources, covering a wide range of inspirational, pastoral, practical and academic subjects. Authors are drawn from many different Christian traditions, and publications aim to meet the needs of a wide variety of readers in the UK and throughout the world.

The Society does not necessarily endorse the individual views contained in its publications, but hopes they stimulate readers to think about and further develop their Christian faith.

For further information about the Society, please write to:

SPCK, Holy Trinity Church, Marylebone Road, London NW1 4DU, United Kingdom.
Telephone: 020 7387 5282